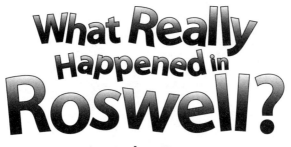

What Really Happened in Roswell?

Just the Facts
(Plus the Rumors)
About UFOs and Aliens

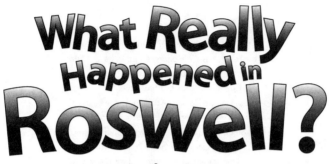

What Really Happened in Roswell?

Just the Facts
(Plus the Rumors)
About UFOs and Aliens

by Kathleen Krull

illustrations by
Christopher Santoro

HarperCollinsPublishers

Library of Congress Cataloging-in-Publication Data
Krull, Kathleen.
What really happened in Roswell? just the facts (plus
the rumors) about UFOs and aliens / by Kathleen Krull ;
illustrations by Christopher Santoro.—1st ed.
   p.   cm.
Summary: Looks into the 1947 crash in New Mexico
of an object which many people believe was an alien
spacecraft, providing reports of what many people claim
to have seen and the government cover-up that followed.
ISBN 0-688-17248-2 (pbk.) — ISBN 0-688-17249-0 (lib. bdg.)
1. Unidentified flying objects—Sightings and encounters—
New Mexico—Roswell—Juvenile literature. [1. Unidentified
flying objects. 2. Extraterrestrial beings. 3. Roswell (N.M.)—
History.] I. Santoro, Christopher, ill. II. Title.
TL789.5.N6 K78 2003   2002014589
001.942'09789'43—dc21   CIP
                                                       AC

Typography by Amy Ryan
1 2 3 4 5 6 7 8 9 10
❖
First Edition

To Cyrus Mayer and his parents,
Aline and Gary
—K.K.

To my editor Mark McVeigh,
whose direction is always inspired
—C.S.

The author would like to thank Ruth Katcher,
as well as Mark McVeigh, Phoebe Yeh,
Sarah Thomson, and Susan Pearson—
genius editors all. Also Pat Laughlin
and Robert Burnham for getting me
to New Mexico and for lots of help
with the research, and Paul
for introducing me to aliens.

Something stunning happened in Roswell, New Mexico, in 1947. This unique incident had to do with aliens. Many stories have been told about it. The book you are holding will reveal:

- **the facts**

- **some of the rumors**

1

Anyone who has ever seen New Mexico knows how out-of-the-ordinary it is. The sky goes on forever—electric blue by day, melting into intense reds and purples at sunset, then a forever of blackness at night. Bleached bones dot the white sand below.

More than fifty years ago, in 1947, towns in New Mexico were few and far between. Even people were few and far between. Water was scarce.

Out in the desert, only the sheep survived, with the help of a few lonely ranchers.

World War II had been over for only two years. It had been the most nightmarish war in history, leaving sixty million people dead. Nations remained tense. The United States and the Soviet Union (known today as Russia) were growing especially chilly toward each other.

The night of June 13, 1947, was like no other night ever. A bizarre event took place in the desert outside the little town of Roswell, New Mexico.

Out of that forever-starry sky, an object fell to the ground.

When something unusual appears in the sky, wild rumors tend to sprout. So soon after World War II, Americans were more nervous than usual. Battles had been won and lost in the skies—mysterious things happened up there. Even balloons were suspicious: Japan had sent balloons with bombs aboard over to California and other western states.

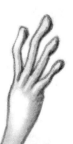

On June 14, eight-year-old Vernon Brazel woke up at dawn. All day long he helped out with chores on his dad's sprawling sheep ranch. His dad, W. W. Brazel, nicknamed Mac, barreled his truck right over the desert sand. Their ranch was so lonely that no roads led to it.

In the late afternoon, Vernon spotted something in the distance. Something gleaming on the ground. What was it?

But Mac wouldn't stop the truck. He was too busy with the daily rounds of the ranch to even pay Vernon much attention.

That night, over a dinner of cold pork and beans and crackers, Mac mentioned Vernon's excitement to

Mrs. Brazel. Vernon's fourteen-year-old sister, Bessie, got excited, too. It didn't really occur to anyone in the family to call the police.

Even if they had wanted to, the Brazels didn't have a phone.

New Mexico played a starring role in World War II. Partly for its isolation, the area known as Los Alamos was chosen as the site of the top-secret Manhattan Project, which was created to develop the atomic bomb. Scientists worked round the clock on the most devastating weapon ever. Not until the United States dropped atomic bombs on Japan to end the war, killing hundreds of thousands, did the rest of the world learn what the Manhattan Project was.

Over the next three weeks, Vernon and Bessie Brazel almost went crazy. They were itching to go back and explore what Vernon had seen.

Finally, on the Fourth of July, Mac took a day off. He drove his family back out into the bleak desert. Vernon pointed the way.

Soon they glimpsed something in the middle of nowhere, some stuff that seemed to have dropped right out of the sky. Vernon and Bessie hopped out and raced around to gather up strange silvery scraps. The mystery material was etched with unearthly writing in pink and purple. Bessie and Vernon tried to make sense of it, gave up, then stuffed the

material into sacks that once con-
tained food for the sheep. Altogether
the sacks weighed about five pounds.

Mac took everyone home. He still
didn't think the whole business was
important enough to report to authorities.

The following morning, Mac had
errands to do in the tiny town of
Corona. While making conversation
with some people he ran into, he
heard a new expression. People were

buzzing about a man up in Washington State who had seen strange "flying disks" in the sky. Mac started to wonder.

A couple of weeks earlier, on June 24, 1947, something jolted a businessman as he flew his private plane. Over Mount Rainier in Washington State, Kenneth Arnold later told newspaper reporters, he saw nine objects flying in formation, moving "like a saucer if you skip it across the water." Newspapers shortened his description, and Arnold became famous as the first person to see "flying saucers." No one has ever identified what Arnold *did* see—tricky clouds, a flock of geese, guided missiles from a nearby army base? The age of UFOs (Unidentified Flying Objects) had officially dawned.

Two days later, Mac had some of his sheeps' wool ready to sell. To get a good price, he drove the truck all the way to Roswell, some one hundred and thirty miles away. Little Roswell was the nearest thing to a big city in that part of New Mexico.

Since he was right there, Mac decided to drop in at the local sheriff's office. At long last, he reported that he and his kids had found some unusual stuff. Could it have come from one of those new "flying disks"?

The sheriff didn't have a clue. He wasn't quite sure *what* to make of Mac's story. To get some advice, he called up the local military authorities at the RAAF, the Roswell Army Air Field.

The next day, the front page of morning newspapers everywhere blasted the news:

Aliens from another planet had landed at Roswell.

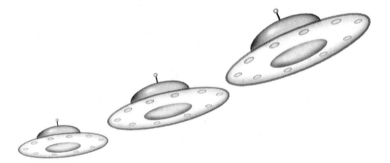

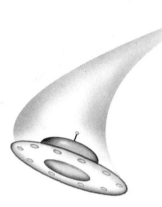

The news reached officials at the U.S. Army headquarters in Washington, D.C. They were not pleased. The army's biggest concern was that people would panic. Panic would cause big headaches, big problems.

According to a newspaper, the army fired off a "blistering" lecture to the RAAF military officers.

In less than twenty-four hours, the RAAF changed its mind about what the Brazels had found in the desert.

Why would the government be so afraid of people panicking? One good reason is something that had happened only nine years earlier. In 1938, a fictional radio broadcast called the "The War of the Worlds" had inspired mass hysteria when some people believed Martians were actually invading New Jersey. No one wanted to repeat this—especially now, in 1947, when our enemy, the Soviet Union, could take advantage of the chaos.

An RAAF general announced that an awful mistake had been made. He said that the bags of mystery material were actually the remains of an ordinary high-altitude balloon used to predict the weather.

Over the radio, the general said, "The wreckage is in my office now and, as far as I can see, there is nothing to get excited about."

Most people quieted down.

One year passed.

By then, the people around Roswell weren't talking much about Mac or Vernon or the flying saucer anymore. So soon after the end of World War II, citizens relied on the government to keep them safe. Almost everyone simply accepted an army general's word. If he said that a flying saucer was really a weather balloon—then that's what it was. The end.

Even as World War II was ending, another sort of war was beginning. The United States and the Soviet Union had been allies against Nazi Germany, but after the war the two superpowers became rivals. It wasn't a raging "hot" war—the two nations never fought directly—but worry rose that one or both *would* start a war. The relationship became like a behind-the-scenes, or "cold," war. So the American government was still in a war mood, especially nervous about weapons the Soviet Union might be secretly developing.

Another year went by.

Like dust whirling in a desert, a rumor came out of nowhere: A flying saucer really *had* landed near Roswell in 1947. People claimed that agents from the U.S. government knew all about it. Agents had even removed alien bodies from the wreck and hidden them away.

The word "cover-up" started to be heard. People were using it to describe the government's explanation about that weather balloon over Roswell.

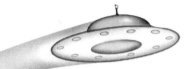

Why would the government cover something up? To protect national security, it does keep secrets from time to time. Most famously—and not so far from Roswell—the Manhattan Project involved some big-time lying. During World War II, the public was not informed that the U.S. was developing the atom bomb. Most people will agree that the research had to be kept secret from America's enemies, but in other situations the debate over national security versus the public's right to know is fierce.

Then, in 1950, a new book came out called *Behind the Flying Saucers*. The author, Frank Scully, claimed that the U.S. Army had not one, not two, but *three* alien spaceships. And a bunch of alien bodies.

There was no evidence to support these claims. That, according to Scully, was because the government was going to a lot of trouble to hide any evidence.

Frank Scully, until he attacked the government in *Behind the Flying Saucers*, was a writer for a Hollywood magazine called *Variety*. Two years later, other journalists revealed that his book was based on a hoax, but by then it was a best-seller.

After this, new people came forward to claim they had seen aliens near Roswell back in 1947. Sometimes they said they saw two of them, sometimes as many as eight. Sometimes the aliens were dead, sometimes still alive. Usually their heads were too big for their small bodies. They had four fingers, large slanted eyes, and tiny ears.

And no hair, no teeth, no toes, and no color in their super-smooth skin.

According to Frank Drake, chairman of the board of trustees of the Search for Extraterrestrial Intelligence (SETI) Institute, the probability that there is other intelligent life in the universe is 100%. The odds that it in any way resembles us? Almost none.

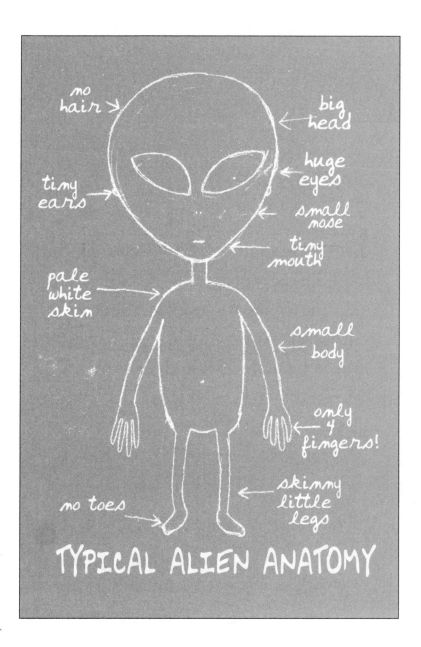

TYPICAL ALIEN ANATOMY

In 1963, many years after making his famous report, Mac Brazel died.

By now, most people didn't talk much about the crash. A few swore they'd been threatened with terrible fates if they revealed what they'd witnessed.

No one knew whether to believe them. After all, it had happened so long ago.

Distrust of government took a leap in the 1960s. America's involvement in the Vietnam War—which lasted from 1955 until 1975—was controversial. Many attacked government decisions, especially those made by the military branch. Then, in 1974, with the incident known as Watergate, President Richard Nixon was forced to resign for attempting to cover up criminal acts. With a loss of confidence in our leaders' words, questions about mysteries like Roswell refused to go away.

In 1980, a new book came out titled *The Roswell Incident* by Charles Berlitz and William L. Moore. It claimed that the government had hidden the truth about the spaceship crash for more than thirty years now.

Like *Behind the Flying Saucers*, this book became a best-seller, too. Many seemed to find it very convincing.

Others noticed that the people who talked the most about Roswell were the ones making the most money—such as with book sales.

Scholars have pointed out that the story of Roswell has a certain familiarity: A bad guy (in this case, the government) hides something essential to humanity (evidence that we are not alone in the universe, or wisdom from other planets). The clever heroes (people searching for the truth) find ways to get around the powerful bad guy. The "truth" can't be proven in any real way, but the heroes get to feel self-righteous, or get rewarded with money. This is the good-versus-evil struggle found in fairy tales and myths all around the world.

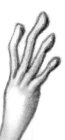

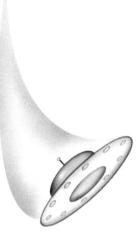

In 1982, a movie called *E.T.: The Extra-Terrestrial* came out. It was about an adorable alien who accidentally gets stranded on Earth and must hide from evil government agents.

E.T. was the biggest hit movie of that year.

Then, in 1993, a new science fiction show called *The X-Files* started on TV. The two FBI agents in the show, Fox Mulder and Dana Scully,

were always insisting that the government had covered up the truth
about Roswell.

The show became wildly popular.

Much specu-
lation takes place about
extraterrestrials visiting Earth, and it
can be hard to remember that no scientif-
ically credible evidence exists that this has
ever happened.

SALE
SPECIAL REPORT
MAN LANDS ON MARS
TV Sale!
$299.00
SPECIAL REPORT
MAN LANDS ON MARS
SPECIAL REPORT
MAN LANDS ON MARS
SPECIAL REPORT
MAN LANDS ON MARS
$816.77

Why did the Roswell story refuse to go away?

Maybe it is human nature to look for patterns (whether they are there or not). In our search for meaning, we like to believe events are not random.

Maybe we are also prone to worrying. Sometimes events seem to take on a hostile pattern—perhaps even a conspiracy.

Americans do love conspiracy theories. Who assassinated President John F. Kennedy and Martin Luther King, Jr.—was it really who the government said it was? Is it possible that frequent sightings of Elvis Presley prove he is still alive, and the government is denying it for some reason? Did American astronauts really walk on the moon in 1969, or is the government only pretending they did? Why was the government always hinting that the Soviet Union was spying on us?

By the 1990s, more and more conspiracy theories were anti-government. For some, the idea of officials conspiring to cover up what has become known as the "Roswell Incident" fit in all too well.

The Roswell story is especially attractive because the questions and the conspiracy possibilities are endless. For example, some people believe even the aliens conspired to hide themselves from earthlings. Why? We don't know, but they never seem to show up in prominent places, such as the White House or the Empire State Building, where their existence could be more easily proven.

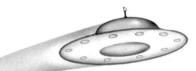

One reason conspiracy theories are so popular is that history occasionally proves them true. During World War II, the government really did keep the Manhattan Project a secret. During the Cold War, the Soviet Union really was spying on us.

Finally, in 1995, the United States Air Force published an extraordinary official report, "The Roswell Report: Fact Versus Fiction in the New Mexico Desert." At long last, it admitted that it *did* lie about the Roswell Incident!

Now the government said that the weather balloon story was in fact a cover-up. The wreckage found by the Brazels, said the report, was really part of a mysterious enterprise called Project MOGUL. This was an ultra-secret mission to spy on the Soviet Union from the upper atmosphere.

The spy balloons of Project MOGUL were like nothing else on earth, according to the report. These balloons were made of aluminum and experimental new materials, all held together with tape. With supplies hard to come by during and after World War II, the government balloons were often manufactured by toy companies; the colorful tape on the Project MOGUL spy balloon was marked with tiny pink and purple images from one such company.

The government report didn't have a thing to say about any alien bodies.

Why would the government cover up Project MOGUL? They said they feared a panic like that caused by "The War of the Worlds" broadcast in 1938 . . . but more sinister theories for the cover-up multiplied.

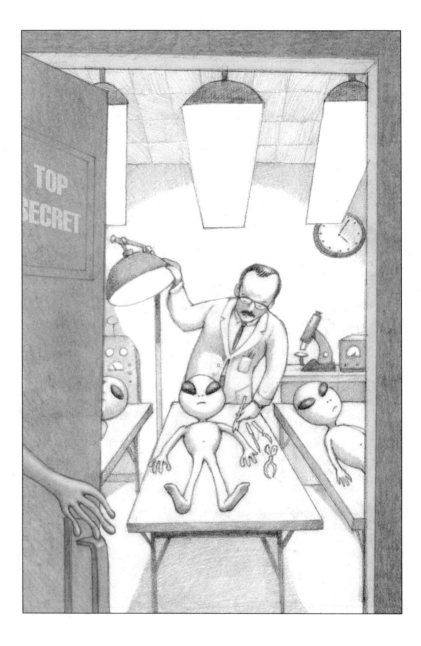

This new information didn't stop the rumors about Roswell.

In 1995, the Fox TV network aired a special called "Alien Autopsy: Fact or Fiction?" Blurry film revealed doctors performing an autopsy on the body of an alien from Roswell. Later, doctors ordered tiny coffins for the aliens.

The show caused a sensation. It became one of the most-watched TV specials ever and even inspired a two-part *The X-Files* episode.

Later that year, it came out that the show was more fiction than fact. It turned out to be a hoax, a publicity stunt.

In 1998, the Fox network aired a show called "World's Greatest Hoaxes: Secrets Finally Re-vealed," featuring none other than its own alien autopsy film.

If anything, speculation about Roswell got even noisier. More and more people who claimed to be witnesses of the crash were coming forward.

So, three years after its first official report about Roswell, the U.S. Air Force spoke up again. Their 1997 book was 231 pages long and was called *The Roswell Report: Case Closed*. It denied once and for all that aliens had crashed at Roswell.

And there were definitely no alien bodies.

Instead, in great detail, the USAF revealed that it had experimented with crash-test dummies. The report said that lots of these fake people were dropped from high altitudes to test what would happen when they hit the ground. Sometimes the dummies got lost in the desert, and they were probably mistaken for aliens.

In 1991, the Soviet Union collapsed, and the Cold War—after more than forty years—was finally over. The American government now saw no harm in making available some of its formerly top-secret information.

The town of Roswell didn't really pay attention to the "Case Closed" report. This was once a poor area. But, by the end of the 1990s, tourists and believers in aliens were spending about five million dollars a year here. For ten dollars, you could even buy a tiny container of dirt from the site of the alien crash.

In July 1997, Roswell threw a huge party to celebrate the fiftieth anniversary of the crash. More than forty thousand people showed up and partied for a week. Aliens appeared on the covers of all the magazines.

After fifty years, Roswell was more important than ever. It was at the heart of claims that aliens have visited earth, the key that held all sorts of UFO believers together.

In the 1990s, President Bill Clinton kept a copy of the USAF Roswell report in his private study in the White House. During the 1999 presidential campaign, a rival candidate joked that Vice President Al Gore was born nine months after the day that aliens landed at Roswell. It was a funny joke, but it's also true: Gore was born on March 31, 1948.

By 1999, some people were taking the Roswell story even further. They decided that it was connected to some of our most incredible scientific advances, that such things as computer chips, cell phones, lasers, and fiber optics could be traced back to technology acquired from the alien spaceship that crashed. Some people believe that the crash had been deliberate: The Roswell aliens "seeded" American companies with their own inventions.

Naturally, the government denies any such thing.

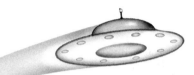

In 1999, multimillionaire Joseph P. Firmage stepped down from his job as the head of USWeb, a high-tech, high-profile company, in order to found the International Space Sciences Organization (ISSO). He intended to focus on alien technology he believed came from the alien spacecraft that crashed at Roswell. "History will be my judge," he said.

As it turned out, that headline from 1947—RAAF CAPTURES FLYING SAUCER ON RANCH IN ROSWELL REGION—was the first and last time in history that the United States officially admitted contact with aliens.

Yet, according to various polls, as many as half of all Americans believe the government is lying. They believe the government knows more than it has disclosed about Roswell, UFOs, and aliens.

Today *any* statement the government makes about Roswell seems suspicious. It can be twisted and used by some as more proof of the greatest cover-up of all time.

And interest in aliens is greater than ever.

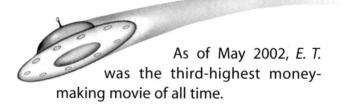

As of May 2002, *E. T.* was the third-highest money-making movie of all time.

Now you have read all the different stories about Roswell. What various people thought, what the government insists is true.

What do *you* believe really happened in Roswell in 1947? And why? What is the truth? And is the story over?

In 2002, the population of Roswell was over fifty thousand and growing.

Sources

Books

Berlitz, Charles, and William L. Moore. *The Roswell Incident,* reissue (New York: Berkley Books, 1991).

Corso, Colonel Philip J., and William Birnes. *The Day After Roswell* (New York: Pocket Books, 1997).

Hepplewhite, Peter, and Neil Tonge. *Alien Encounters* (New York: Sterling, 1997).

Jung, C. G. *Flying Saucers: A Modern Myth of Things Seen in the Sky* (New York: Harcourt, 1959).

Klass, Philip J. *The Real Roswell Crashed-Saucer Coverup* (Amherst, NY: Prometheus Books, 1997).

Mitton, Jacqueline. *Informania Aliens* (Cambridge, MA: Candlewick, 1999).

Randle, Kevin D., and Donald R. Schmitt. *The Truth About the UFO Crash at Roswell* (New York: Avon Books, 1994).

Sagan, Carl. *The Demon-Haunted World: Science as a Candle in the Dark* (New York: Random House, 1995).

Saler, Benson, and Charles A. Ziegler and Charles B. Moore. *UFO Crash at Roswell: The Genesis of a Modern Myth* (Washington, D.C.: Smithsonian Institution Press, 1997).

Scully, Frank. *Behind the Flying Saucers* (New York: Holt, 1950).

Shermer, Michael. *Why People Believe Weird Things* (New York: W. H. Freeman, 1997).

Websites

USAF "The Roswell Report:
Case Closed"—
www.af.mil/lib/roswell
Albuquerque Journal section
devoted to Roswell—
www.abqjournal.com/roswell
Center for UFO Studies—
www.cufos.org
International UFO Museum
and Research Center—
www.iufomrc.org
Search for Extraterrestrial
Intelligence (SETI) Institute—
www.seti-inst.edu

Watch the skies—
and your local bookstore—
for a fresh look
at another alien mystery:

The Night the Martians Landed

Just the Facts
(Plus the Rumors)
About Invaders from Mars

by Kathleen Krull

illustrations by
Christopher Santoro

A funny account of a radio broadcast about a Martian invasion that was so realistic it fooled the nation.

Arriving on Earth in August 2003.

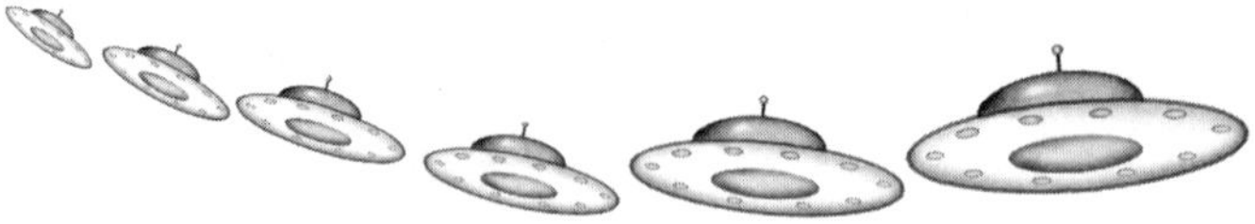
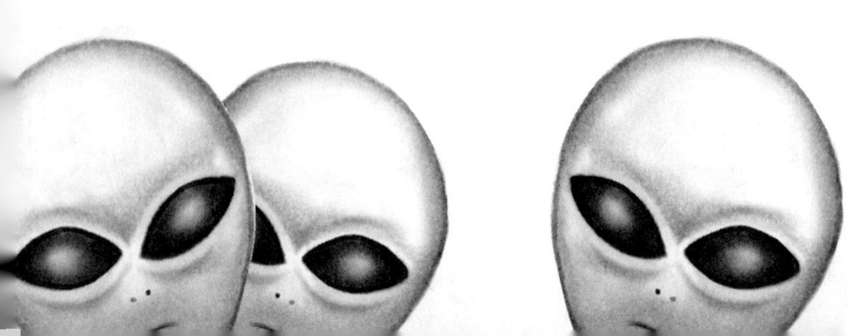